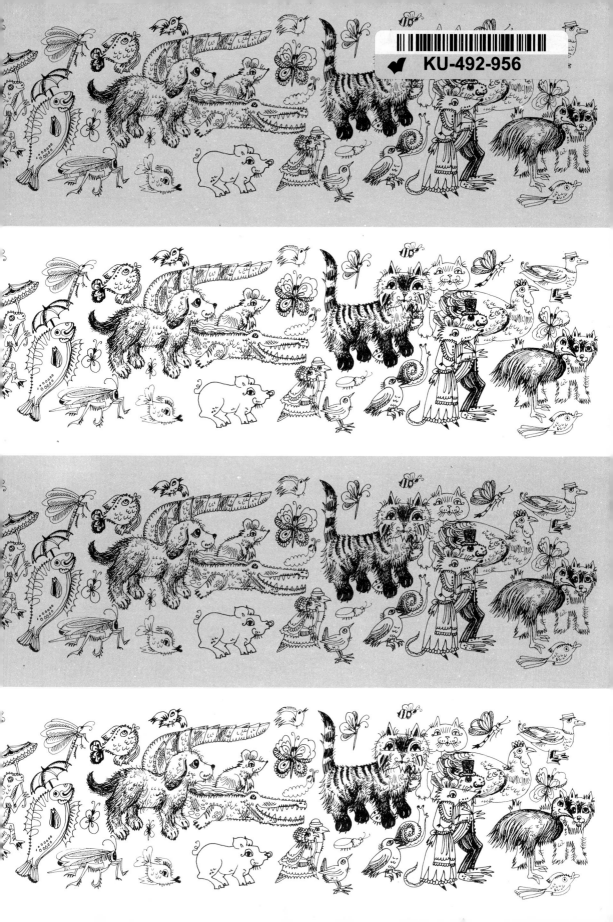

If You Should Meet a Crocodile

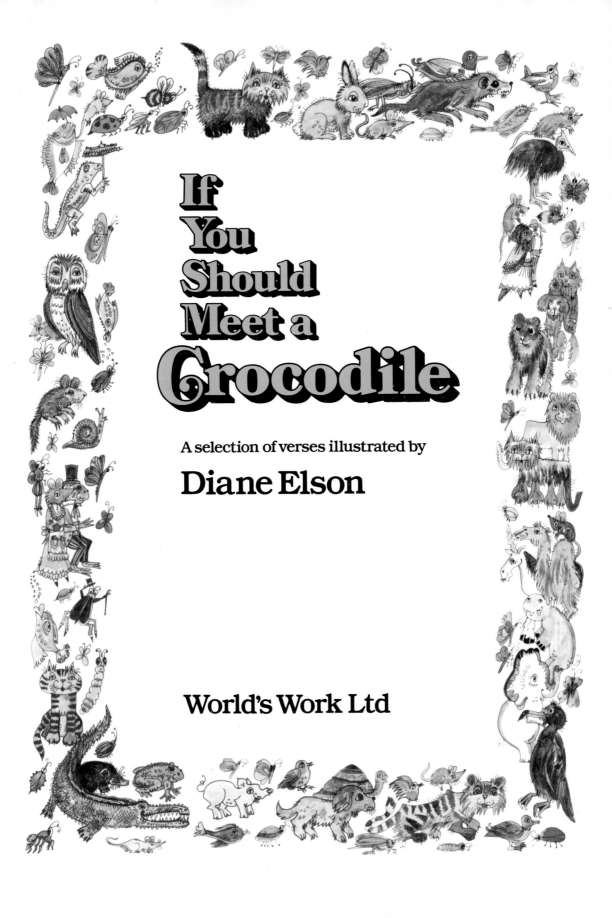

If You Should Meet a Crocodile

A selection of verses illustrated by

Diane Elson

World's Work Ltd

Illustrations copyright © 1979 by Diane Elson
Published in 1979 by
World's Work Ltd
The Windmill Press Kingswood Tadworth, Surrey
Reproduced by Graphic Affairs, Southend, Essex
Printed by offset in Great Britain by
Fakenham Press Limited, Fakenham, Norfolk

SBN 437 37702 4

Puss came dancing out of a barn
With a pair of bagpipes under her arm;
She could sing nothing but, Fiddle cum fee,
The mouse has married the humble-bee.
Pipe, cat—dance, mouse—
We'll have a wedding at our good house.

As I was going to St. Ives,
I met a man with seven wives;
Each wife had seven sacks,
Each sack had seven cats,
Each cat had seven kits:
Kits, cats, sacks, and wives,
How many were there going
to St. Ives?

[One or None]

Where are you going,
My little cat?

I am going to town,
To get me a hat.

What! a hat for a cat!
A cat get a hat!
Who ever saw a cat with a hat?

Eliza Lee Follen

Five little pussy cats sitting in a row,
Blue ribbons round each neck, fastened in a bow.
Hey pussies! Ho pussies! Are your faces clean?
Don't you know you're sitting there so as to be seen.

Pussy at the fireside suppin' up brose,
Down came a cinder and burned pussy's nose.
Oh, said pussy, that's no fair.
Well, said the cinder, you shouldn't be there.

Pussy cat, pussy cat, where have you been?
I've been to London to look at the Queen.

Pussy cat, pussy cat, what did you there?
I frightened a little mouse under her chair.

Rat a tat tat, who is that?
Only grandma's pussy cat.
What do you want?
A pint of milk.
Where's your money?
In my pocket.
Where's your pocket?
I forgot it.
O you silly pussy cat!

Where are you going,
My little kittens?

We are going to town
To get us some mittens.

What! mittens for kittens!
Do kittens wear mittens?
Who ever saw little kittens with mittens?

Eliza Lee Follen

Ding, dong, bell,
Pussy's in the well.
Who put her in?
Little Johnny Green.
Who pulled her out?
Little Tommy Stout.
What a naughty boy was that
To try to drown poor pussy cat,
Who never did him any harm,
And killed the mice in his father's barn.

Pussy cat Mole jumped over a coal
And in her best petticoat burnt a great hole.
Poor pussy's weeping, she'll have no more milk
Until her best petticoat's mended with silk.

Hey diddle, diddle,
The cat and the fiddle,
The cow jumped over the moon;
The little dog laughed
To see such sport,
And the dish ran away with the spoon.

The Owl and the Pussy-cat

The Owl and the Pussy-cat went to sea
    In a beautiful pea-green boat,
They took some honey, and plenty of money,
    Wrapped up in a five-pound note.
The Owl looked up to the stars above,
    And sang to a small guitar,
'O lovely Pussy! O Pussy, my love,
    What a beautiful Pussy you are,
        You are,
        You are!
What a beautiful Pussy you are!'

Pussy said to the Owl, 'You elegant fowl!
    How charmingly sweet you sing!
O let us be married! too long we have tarried:
    But what shall we do for a ring?'
They sailed away, for a year and a day,
    To the land where the Bong-tree grows,
And there in a wood a Piggy-wig stood
    With a ring at the end of his nose,
        His nose,
        His nose,
    With a ring at the end of his nose.

'Dear Pig, are you willing to sell for one shilling
    Your ring?' Said the Piggy, 'I will.'
So they took it away, and were married next day
    By the Turkey who lives on the hill.
They dined on mince, and slices of quince,
    Which they ate with a runcible spoon;
And hand in hand, on the edge of the sand,
    They danced by the light of the moon,
        The moon,
        The moon,
    They danced by the light of the moon.

Edward Lear

A wise old owl sat in an oak,
The more he heard the less he spoke;
The less he spoke the more he heard.
Why aren't we all like that wise old bird?

I saw eight magpies in a tree.
Two for you and six for me:

One for sorrow,
        two for mirth,
Three for a wedding,
        four for a birth:

Five for England,
        six for France,
Seven for a fiddler,
        eight for a dance.

The Wren

The little Wren of tender mind,
To every other bird is kind;
It ne'er to mischief bends its will,
But sings and is good-humoured still.
Whoe'er has mixed in childish play
Must sure have heard the children say,
'The Robin and the Jenny Wren
Are God Almighty's cock and hen.'
Hence 'tis from all respect they meet,
Hence all in kindly manner treat;
For none would use with disrespect,
Whom Heaven thinks proper to protect.

The Autumn Robin

Sweet little bird in russet coat,
    The livery of the closing year,
I love thy lonely plaintive note
    And tiny whispering song to hear,
While on the stile or garden seat
    I sit to watch the falling leaves,
The song thy little joys repeat
    My loneliness relieves.

John Clare

The common cormorant or shag
Lays eggs inside a paper bag
The reason you will see no doubt
It is to keep the lightning out
But what these unobservant birds
Have never noticed is that herds
Of wandering bears may come with buns
And steal the bags to hold the crumbs.

Mr. and Mrs. Spikky Sparrow

On a little piece of wood,
Mr. Spikky Sparrow stood;
Mrs. Sparrow sate close by,
A-making of an insect pie,
For her little children five,
In the nest and all alive,
Singing with a cheerful smile
To amuse them all the while,
    Twikky wikky wikky wee,
    Wikky bikky twikky tee,
     Spikky bikky bee!

Mrs. Spikky Sparrow said,
'Spikky, darling! in my head
Many thoughts of trouble come,
Like to flies upon a plum!
All last night, among the trees,
I heard you cough, I heard you sneeze;
And, thought I, it's come to that
Because he does not wear a hat!
    Chippy wippy sikky tee!
    Bikky wikky tikky mee!
     Spikky chippy wee!

'Not that you are growing old,
But the nights are growing cold.
No one stays out all night long
Without a hat: I'm sure it's wrong!'
Mr. Spikky said, 'How kind,
Dear, you are, to speak your mind!
All your life I wish you luck!
You are! you are! a lovely duck!
      Witchy witchy witchy wee!
      Twitchy witchy witchy bee!
        Tikky tikky tee!

'I was also sad, and thinking,
When one day I saw you winking,
And I heard you sniffle-snuffle,
And I saw your feathers ruffle;
To myself I sadly said,
She's neuralgia in her head!
That dear head has nothing on it!
Ought she not to wear a bonnet?
      Witchy kitchy kitchy wee?
      Spikky wikky mikky bee?
        Chippy wippy chee?

'Let us both fly up to town!
There I'll buy you such a gown!
Which, completely in the fashion,
You shall tie a sky-blue sash on.
And a pair of slippers neat,
To fit your darling little feet,
So that you will look and feel
Quite galloobious and genteel!
  Jikky wikky bikky see,
    Chicky bikky wikky bee,
      Twicky witchy wee!'

So they both to London went,
Alighting on the Monument,
Whence they flew down swiftly—pop,
Into Moses' wholesale shop;
There they bought a hat and bonnet,
And a gown with spots upon it,
A satin sash of Cloxam blue,
And a pair of slippers too.
    Zikky wikky mikky bee,
    Witchy witchy mitchy kee,
        Sikky tikky wee.

Then when so completely drest,
Back they flew, and reached their nest.
Their children cried, 'O Ma and Pa!
How truly beautiful you are!'
Said they, 'We trust that cold or pain
We shall never feel again!
While, perched on tree, or house, or steeple,
We now shall look like other people.
    Witchy witchy witchy wee,
    Twikky mikky bikky bee,
        Zikky sikky tee.'

Edward Lear

Hickety, pickety, my black hen,
She lays eggs for gentlemen;
Gentlemen come every day
To see what my black hen doth lay.

If I were a cassowary
On the plains of Timbuctoo,
I would eat a missionary,
Cassock, bands, and hymn-book too.

Bishop Samuel Wilberforce

32

The Canary

Mary had a little bird,
    With feathers bright and yellow.
Slender legs—upon my word,
    He was a pretty fellow!

Sweetest notes he always sung,
    Which much delighted Mary;
Often where his cage was hung,
    She sat to hear Canary.

Crumbs of bread and dainty seeds
    She carried to him daily,
Seeking for the early weeds,
    She decked his palace gaily.

This, my little readers, learn,
    And ever practice duly;
Songs and smiles of love return
    To friends who love you truly.

Elizabeth Turner

Little Trotty Wagtail

Little Trotty Wagtail, he went in the rain,
And twittering, tottering sideways he ne'er got
    straight again.
He stooped to get a worm, and looked up to get a fly,
And then he flew away ere his feathers they were dry.

Little Trotty Wagtail, he waddled in the mud,
And left his little footmarks, trample where he would.
He waddled in the water-pudge, and waggle went his tail.
And chirrupt up his wings to dry upon the garden rail.

Little Trotty Wagtail, you nimble all about,
And in the dimpling water-pudge you waddle in and out;
Your home is nigh at hand, and in the warm pig stye,
So, little Master Wagtail, I'll bid you a good-bye.

John Clare

Three young rats with black felt hats,
Three young ducks with white straw flats,
Three young dogs with curling tails,
Three young cats with demi-veils,
Went out to walk with two young pigs
In satin vests and sorrel wigs;
But suddenly it chanced to rain
And so they all went home again.

The Tale of a Dog and a Bee

Great big dog,
Head upon his toes;
Tiny little bee
Settles on his nose.

Great big dog
Thinks it is a fly.
Never says a word,
Winks very sly.

Tiny little bee,
Tickles dog's nose—
Thinks like as not
'Tis a pretty rose.

Dog smiles a smile,
Winks his other eye,
Chuckles to himself
How he'll catch a fly.

Then he makes a snap,
Very quick and spry,
Does his level best,
But doesn't catch the fly.

Tiny little bee,
Alive and looking well;
Great big dog,
Mostly gone to swell.

Moral:
Dear friends and brothers all,
Don't be too fast and free,
And when you catch a fly,
Be sure it's not a bee.

Two little Dogs went out for a walk,
    And it was windy weather,
So for fear the wind should blow them away,
    They tied their tails together.

They tied their tails with a yard of tape,
    And the wind it blew and blew
As sharp and keen as a carving-knife,
    And cut the tape in two.

And away and away, like kites in the air
    Those two little Dogs flew about,
Till one little Dog was blown to bits,
    And the other turned inside out.

D'Arcy Wentworth Thompson

I had a little dog and his name was Blue Bell,
I gave him some work, and he did it very well;
I sent him upstairs to pick up a pin,
He stepped in the coal-scuttle up to his chin;
I sent him to the garden to pick some sage,
He tumbled down and fell in a rage;
I sent him to the cellar to draw a pot of beer,
He came up again and said there was none there.

There was an Old Man of Ancona,
Who found a small Dog with no Owner,
    Which he took up and down
    All the streets of the town;
That anxious Old Man of Ancona.

Edward Lear

Hoddley, poddley, puddle and fogs,
Cats are to marry the poodle dogs;
Cats in blue jackets and dogs in red hats,
What will become of the mice and the rats?

The lion and the unicorn
　　Were fighting for the crown;
The lion beat the unicorn
　　All around the town.

Some gave them white bread,
　　And some gave them brown;
Some gave them plum cake
　　And drummed them out of town.

The Camel's Complaint

Canary-birds feed on sugar and seed,
    Parrots have crackers to crunch;
And as for the poodles, they tell me the noodles
    Have chicken and cream for their lunch.
        But there's never a question
        About my digestion—
        Anything does for me.

Cats, you're aware, can repose in a chair,
    Chickens can roost upon rails;
Puppies are able to sleep in a stable,
    And oysters can slumber in pails.
        But no one supposes
        A poor camel dozes—
        Any place does for me.

Lambs are enclosed where it's never exposed,
    Coops are constructed for hens;
Kittens are treated to houses well heated,
    And pigs are protected by pens.
        But a camel comes handy
        Wherever it's sandy—
        Anywhere does for me.

People would laugh if you rode a giraffe,
 Or mounted the back of an ox;
It's nobody's habit to ride on a rabbit,
 Or try to bestraddle a fox.
  But as for a camel, he's
  Ridden by families—
  Any load does for me.

A snake is as round as a hole in the ground,
And weasels are wavy and sleek;
And no alligator could ever be straighter
Than lizards that live in a creek.
But a camel's all lumpy
And bumpy and humpy—
Any shape does for me.

Charles E. Carryl

43

Calico Pie
Calico Pie,
The little Birds fly
Down to the calico tree,
Their wings were blue,
And they sang 'Tilly-loo!'
Till away they flew—
    And they never came back to me!
        They never came back!
        They never came back!
    They never came back to me!

Calico Jam,
The little Fish swam,
Over the syllabub sea,
He took off his hat,
To the Sole and the Sprat,
And the Willeby-wat,—
    But he never came back to me!
        He never came back!
        He never came back!
    He never came back to me!

Calico Ban,
The little Mice ran,
To be ready in time for tea,
Flippity flup,
They drank it all up,
And danced in the cup,—
    But they never came back to me!
      They never came back!
      They never came back!
    They never came back to me!

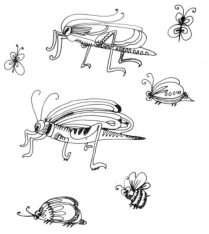

Calico Drum,
The Grasshoppers come,
The Butterfly, Beetle, and Bee,
Over the ground,
Around and around,
With a hop and a bound,—
    But they never came back!
      They never came back!
      They never came back!
    They never came back to me!   *Edward Lear*

The City Mouse and the Garden Mouse

The city mouse lives in a house;
    The garden mouse lives in a bower,
He's friendly with the frogs and toads,
    And sees the pretty plants in flower.

The city mouse eats bread and cheese;
   The garden mouse eats what he can;
We will not grudge him seeds and stocks,
   Poor little timid furry man.

Christina Rossetti

The Mad Gardener's Song

He thought he saw an Elephant,
    That practised on a fife:
He looked again, and found it was
    A letter from his wife.
'At length I realise,' he said,
    'The bitterness of Life!'

He thought he saw a Buffalo
　　Upon the chimney-piece:
He looked again, and found it was
　　His Sister's Husband's Niece.
'Unless you leave this house,' he said,
　　'I'll send for the Police!'

He thought he saw a Rattlesnake
　　That questioned him in Greek:
He looked again, and found it was
　　The Middle of Next Week.
'The one thing I regret,' he said,
　　'Is that it cannot speak!'

He thought he saw a Banker's Clerk
    Descending from the bus:
He looked again, and found it was
    A Hippopotamus:
'If this should stay to dine,' he said,
    'There won't be much for us!'

He thought he saw a Kangaroo
    That worked a coffee-mill:
He looked again, and found it was
    A Vegetable-Pill.
'Were I to swallow this,' he said,
    'I should be very ill!'

He thought he saw a Coach-and-Four
    That stood beside his bed:
He looked again, and found it was
    A Bear without a Head.
'Poor thing,' he said, 'poor silly thing!
    It's waiting to be fed!'

He thought he saw an Albatross
    That fluttered round the lamp:
He looked again, and found it was
    A Penny-Postage-Stamp.
'You'd best be getting home,' he said:
    'The nights are very damp!'

He thought he saw a Garden-Door
    That opened with a key:
He looked again, and found it was
    A Double Rule of Three:
'And all its mystery,' he said,
    'Is clear as day to me!'

He thought he saw an Argument
    That proved he was the Pope:
He looked again, and found it was
    A Bar of Mottled Soap.
'A fact so dread,' he faintly said,
    'Extinguishes all hope!'

Lewis Carroll

One old Oxford ox opening oysters;

Two tee-totums totally tired of trying to trot to Tadbury;

Three tall tigers tippling tenpenny tea;

Four fat friars fanning fainting flies;

Five frippy Frenchmen foolishly fishing for flies;

Six sportsmen shooting snipes;

Seven Severn salmons swallowing shrimps;

Eight Englishmen eagerly examining Europe;

Nine nimble noblemen nibbling nonpareils;

Ten tinkers tinkling upon ten tin tinder-boxes
with ten tenpenny tacks;

Eleven elephants elegantly equipt;

Twelve typographical topographers typically translating types.

There was an Old Person of Ickley,
Who could not abide to ride quickly;
    He rode to Karnak
    On a Tortoise's back,
That moony Old Person of Ickley.

Edward Lear

There was an Old Person of Bray,
Who sang through the whole of the Day
    To his Ducks and his Pigs,
    Whom he fed upon Figs,
That valuable Person of Bray.

Edward Lear

This is the house that Jack built.

This is the malt
That lay in the house that Jack built.

This is the rat,
That ate the malt
That lay in the house that Jack built.

This is the cat,
That killed the rat,
That ate the malt
That lay in the house that Jack built.

This is the dog,
That worried the cat,
That killed the rat,
That ate the malt
That lay in the house that Jack built.

This is the cow with the crumpled horn,
That tossed the dog,
That worried the cat,
That killed the rat,
That ate the malt
That lay in the house that Jack built.

This is the maiden all forlorn,
That milked the cow with the crumpled horn,
That tossed the dog,
That worried the cat,
That killed the rat,
That ate the malt
That lay in the house that Jack built.

This is the man all tattered and torn,
That kissed the maiden all forlorn,
That milked the cow with the crumpled horn,
That tossed the dog,
That worried the cat,
That killed the rat,
That ate the malt
That lay in the house that Jack built.

This is the priest all shaven and shorn,
That married the man all tattered and torn,
That kissed the maiden all forlorn,
That milked the cow with the crumpled horn,
That tossed the dog,
That worried the cat,
That killed the rat,
That ate the malt
That lay in the house that Jack built.

This is the cock that crowed in the morn,
That waked the priest all shaven and shorn,
That married the man all tattered and torn,
That kissed the maiden all forlorn,
That milked the cow with the crumpled horn,
That tossed the dog,
That worried the cat,
That killed the rat,
That ate the malt
That lay in the house that Jack built.

This is the farmer sowing his corn,
That kept the cock that crowed in the morn,
That waked the priest all shaven and shorn,
That married the man all tattered and torn,
That kissed the maiden all forlorn,
That milked the cow with the crumpled horn,
That tossed the dog,
That worried the cat,
That killed the rat,
That ate the malt
That lay in the house that Jack built.

This is the horse and the hound and the horn,
That belonged to the farmer sowing his corn,
That kept the cock that crowed in the morn,
That waked the priest all shaven and shorn,
That married the man all tattered and torn,
That kissed the maiden all forlorn,
That milked the cow with the crumpled horn,
That tossed the dog,
That worried the cat,
That killed the rat,
That ate the malt
That lay in the house that Jack built.

If I had a donkey that wouldn't go,
Would I beat him? Oh no, no.
I'd put him in the barn and give him some corn,
The best little donkey that ever was born.

The Lobster

'Tis the voice of the Lobster: I heard him declare,
'You have baked me too brown, I must sugar my hair.'
As a duck with its eyelids, so he with his nose
Trims his belt and his buttons, and turns out his toes.

I passed by his garden, and marked, with one eye,
How the Owl and the Oyster were sharing a pie;
While the Duck and the Dodo, the Lizard and Cat,
Were swimming in milk round the brim of a hat.

Lewis Carroll

When fishes set umbrellas up
If the rain-drops run,
Lizards will want their parasols
To shade them from the sun.

The peacock has a score of eyes,
    With which he cannot see;
The cod-fish has a silent sound,
    However that may be.

No dandelions tell the time,
    Although they turn to clocks;
Cat's cradle does not hold the cat,
    Nor foxglove fit the fox.

Christina Rossetti

The Snail

To grass, or leaf, or fruit, or wall,
The Snail sticks close, nor fears to fall,
As if he grew there, house and all
                Together.

Within that house secure he hides,
When danger imminent betides
Of storms, or other harm besides,
              Of weather.

Give but his horns the slightest touch,
His self-collecting power is such,
He shrinks into his house with much
              Displeasure.

Where'er he dwells, he dwells alone,
Except himself has chattels none,
Well satisfied to be his own
                    Whole treasure.

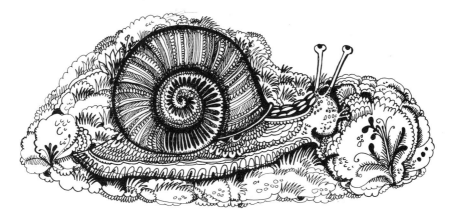

Thus hermit-like, his life he leads,
Nor partner of his Banquet needs,
And if he meets one, only feeds
                    The faster.

Who seeks him must be worse than blind
(He and his house are so combined)
If, finding it, he fails to find
                    Its master.

William Cowper

Fiddle-de-dee, fiddle-de-dee,
The fly shall marry the humble-bee.
They went to church, and married was she.
The fly has married the humble-bee.

Bless you, bless you, burnie-bee,
Tell me when my wedding be;
If it be tomorrow day,
Take your wings and fly away.
Fly to the east, fly to the west,
Fly to him I love the best.

Up and down the City Road,
    In and out the Eagle,
That's the way the money goes,
    Pop goes the weasel!

Half a pound of tuppenny rice,
    Half a pound of treacle,
Mix it up and make it nice,
    Pop goes the weasel!

Every night when I go out
    The monkey's on the table;
Take a stick and knock it off,
    Pop goes the weasel!

CITY ROAD

TREACLE

RICE

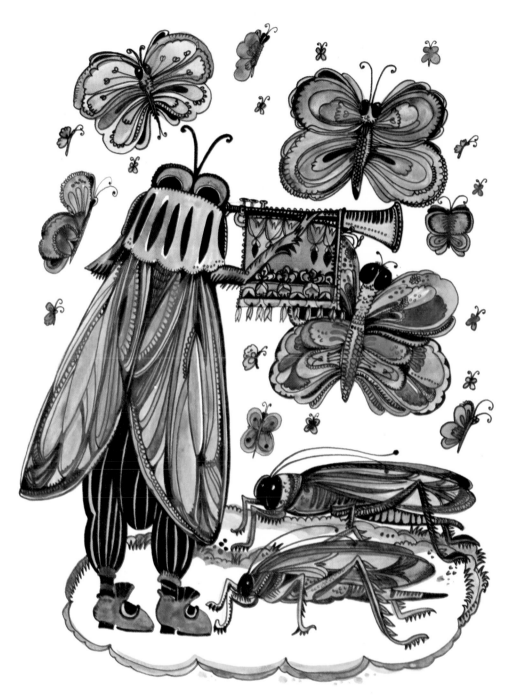

The Butterfly's Ball

Come take up your hats, and away let us haste,
To the Butterfly's Ball, and the Grasshopper's Feast.
The trumpeter Gadfly has summoned the crew,
And the revels are now only waiting for you.

On the smooth-shaven grass by the side of a wood,
Beneath a broad oak which for ages has stood,
See the children of earth and the tenants of air,
For an evening's amusement together repair.

And there came the Beetle, so blind and so black,
Who carried the Emmet, his friend, on his back.

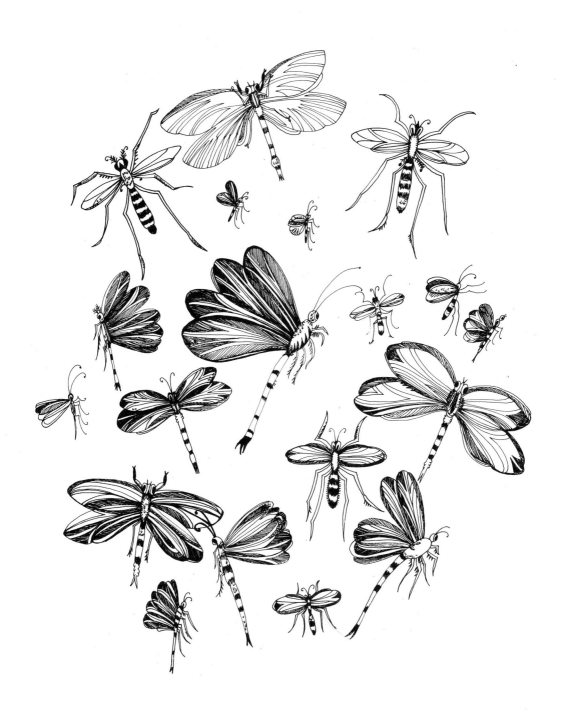

And there came the Gnat, and the Dragonfly too,
And all their relations, green, orange, and blue.

And there came the Moth, with her plumage of down,
And the Hornet, with jacket of yellow and brown;
Who with him the Wasp, his companion, did bring,
But they promised that evening, to lay by their sting.

Then the sly little Dormouse crept out of his hole,
And led to the feast his blind cousin the Mole.
And the Snail, with his horns peeping out of his shell,
Came, fatigued with the distance, the length of an ell.

A mushroom their table, and on it was laid
A water-dock leaf, which a tablecloth made.
The viands were various, to each of their taste,
And the Bee brought the honey to sweeten the feast.

With steps most majestic the Snail did advance,
And he promised the gazers a minuet to dance;
But they all laughed so loud that he drew in his head,
And went in his own little chamber to bed.

Then, as evening gave way to the shadows of night,
Their watchman, the Glow-worm, came out with his light.
So home let us hasten, while yet we can see;
For no watchman is waiting for you and for me.

William Roscoe

Said a frog on a log,
　　'Listen, little Bunny.
Will you ride by my side?
　　Wouldn't that be funny!'

A frog he would a-wooing go,
    Heigh ho! says Rowley,
Whether his mother would let him or no.
    With a rowley, powley, gammon and spinach,
    Heigh ho! says Anthony Rowley.

So off he set with his opera hat,
Heigh ho! says Rowley,
And on the road he met with a rat.
With a rowley, powley, gammon and spinach,
Heigh ho! says Anthony Rowley.

Pray, Mister Rat, will you go with me?
Heigh ho! says Rowley,
Kind Mistress Mousey for to see?
With a rowley, powley, gammon and spinach,
Heigh ho! says Anthony Rowley.

They came to the door of Mousey's hall,
     Heigh ho! says Rowley,
They gave a loud knock, and they gave a loud call.
     With a rowley, powley, gammon and spinach,
     Heigh ho! says Anthony Rowley.

Pray, Mistress Mouse, are you within?
     Heigh ho! says Rowley,
Oh yes, kind sirs, I'm sitting to spin.
     With a rowley, powley, gammon and spinach,
     Heigh ho! says Anthony Rowley.

Pray, Mistress Mouse, will you give us some beer?
  Heigh ho! says Rowley,
For Froggy and I are fond of good cheer.
  With a rowley, powley, gammon and spinach,
  Heigh ho! says Anthony Rowley.

Pray, Mister Frog, will you give us a song?
    Heigh ho! says Rowley,
Let it be something that's not very long.
    With a rowley, powley, gammon and spinach,
    Heigh ho! says Anthony Rowley.

Indeed, Mistress Mouse, replied Mister Frog,
    Heigh ho! says Rowley,
A cold has made me as hoarse as a dog.
    With a rowley, powley, gammon and spinach,
    Heigh ho! says Anthony Rowley.

Since you have a cold, Mister Frog, Mousey said,
    Heigh ho! says Rowley,
I'll sing you a song that I have just made.
    With a rowley, powley, gammon and spinach,
    Heigh ho! says Anthony Rowley.

But while they were all a-merry-making,
Heigh ho! says Rowley,

A cat and her kittens came tumbling in.
With a rowley, powley, gammon and spinach,
Heigh ho! says Anthony Rowley.

The cat she seized the rat by the crown,
  Heigh ho! says Rowley,

93

The kittens they pulled the little mouse down.
  With a rowley, powley, gammon and spinach,
  Heigh ho! says Anthony Rowley.

This put Mister Frog in a terrible fright,
　　Heigh ho! says Rowley,
He took up his hat and he wished them good-night.
　　With a rowley, powley, gammon and spinach,
　　Heigh ho! says Anthony Rowley.

But as Froggy was crossing over a brook,
  Heigh ho! says Rowley,
A lily-white duck came and gobbled him up.
  With a rowley, powley, gammon and spinach,
  Heigh ho! says Anthony Rowley.

So there was an end of one, two, three,
    Heigh ho! says Rowley,
The rat, the mouse, and the little frog-ee.

With a rowley, powley, gammon and spinach,
Heigh ho! says Anthony Rowley.

If you should meet a crocodile,
    Don't take a stick and poke him;
Ignore the welcome in his smile,
    Be careful not to stroke him.

For as he sleeps upon the Nile,
    He thinner gets and thinner;
And whene'er you meet a crocodile
    He's ready for his dinner.

One morning a weasel came swimming
All the way over from France,
And taught all the weasels of England
To play on the fiddle and dance.

There was a little guinea-pig,
Who, being little, was not big;
He always walked upon his feet,
And never fasted when he eat.

When from a place he ran away,
He never at that place did stay;
And while he ran, as I am told,
He ne'er stood still for young or old.

He often squeaked and sometimes vi'lent,
And when he squeaked he ne'er was silent;
Though ne'er instructed by a cat,
He knew a mouse was not a rat.

One day, as I am certified,
He took a whim and fairly died;
And as I'm told by men of sense,
He never has been living since.

Six little mice sat down to spin;
Pussy passed by and she peeped in.
What are you doing, my little men?
Weaving coats for gentlemen.
Shall I come in and cut off your threads?
No, no, Mistress Pussy, you'd bite off our heads.
Oh, no, I'll not; I'll help you to spin.
That may be so, but you don't come in.

I saw a ship a-sailing,
    A-sailing on the sea,
And oh, but it was laden
    With pretty things for thee!

There were comfits in the cabin,
    And apples in the hold;
The sails were made of silk,
    And the masts were all of gold.

The four-and-twenty sailors,
    That stood between the decks,
Were four-and-twenty white mice
    With chains about their necks.

The captain was a duck
    With a packet on his back,
And when the ship began to move
    The captain said, Quack! Quack!

Index of first lines